Pale Sun Shining

The Author

Neil's poetry tends not to rhyme.

He has often wondered if he should say sorry for that.

But, no, they are what they are.

He may say his main influences are Philip Larkin and Wallace Stevens,

but in the main he just sits there and writes.

"Just about things. That were there.

Things. They are always there."

Neil Rigby

Pale Sun Shining

t

totem

Published in London in 2016
by Totem
60 Swinley House Redhill Street,
London NW1 4BB

Title: Pale Sun Shining
Form: Poetry
Author: Neil Rigby
Author's Nationality: British

ISBN: 978-1-899151-09-7

Designed and Typeset by Ishmael Annobil
Cover and interior illustrations by Ishmael Annobil

LIST OF CONTENTS

My thanks go to Ishmael,
who as one of those things, has always been there.
And Tara. And Isabella. And Sophia.

The world is grown so bad, that wrens make prey where eagles dare not perch.
- Shakespeare, Richard III

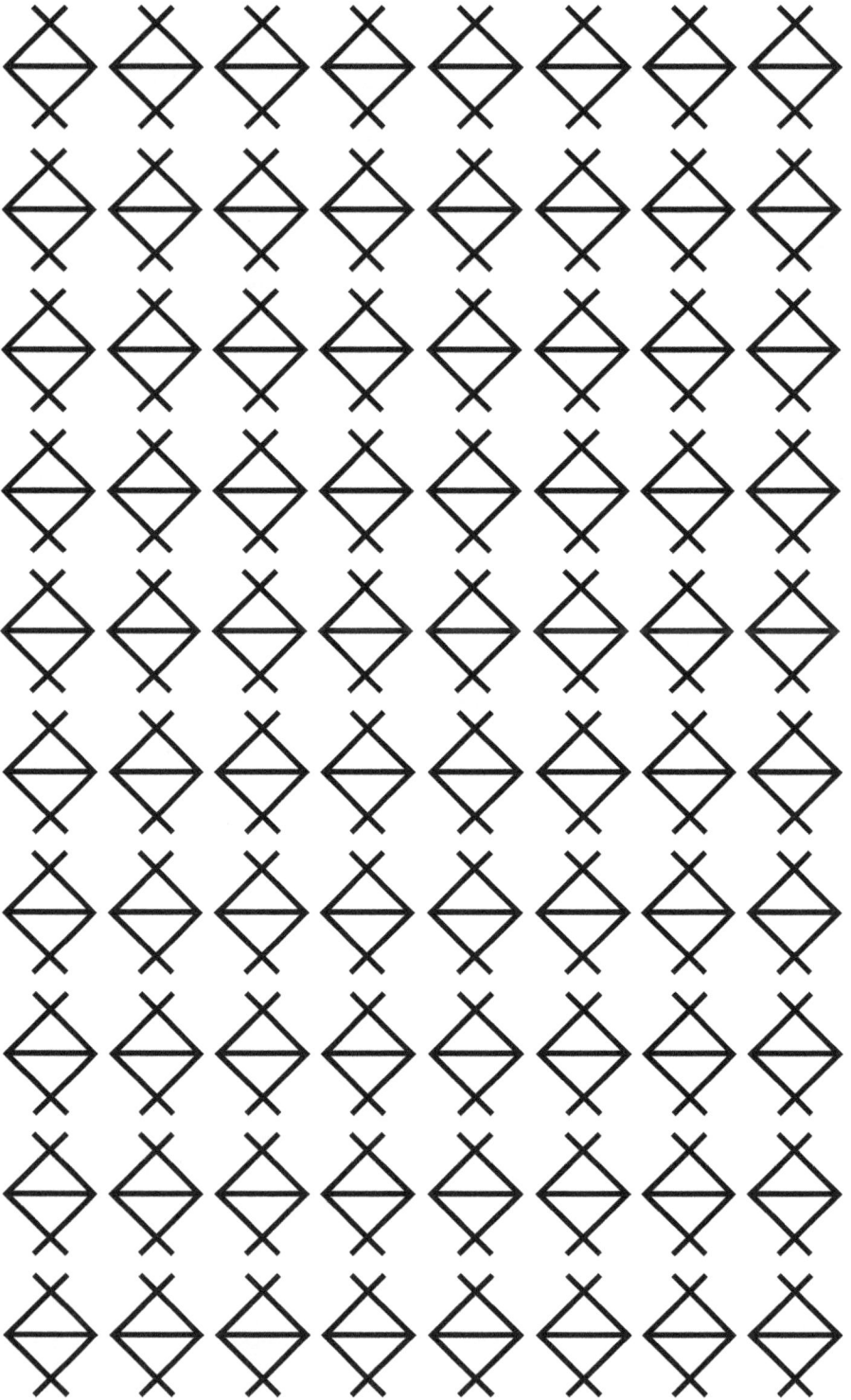

To my dad, Graham.
See you when I see you.

A Ripping Yarn

This is different paraphernalia and I am now
A moving target, shifting for affect, the result aesthetic.

Dust in a room with the only penchant a sliver
Of sunlight, beaming a cutting edge, I redeem these

Dark borders, they're a comfort blanket, completed with
Tunnel vision the blinking, silent eyes take all with them

Into an abyss.

I surface, those films where Hero bursts out
From under sea waves, coughing and spluttering lungs

And gasping for air.

So the surroundings change and I strain for their
Echoes inside, a game worth playing from time to time

But the clamour and crap persist and the driving rain
Will always promise to wash clean and yet leave its victims dank.

It's been like this a while now, seems I'm now
A moving target, shifting my affects, the result aesthetic.

Come Inside and Try

Inanity butchers the fragile shell
And renders the pieces inconstant.
My head feels empty and devoid
Of the chains I enjoy in moments

That come infrequently enough to bear.
Give me time and I will paint with
Tainted brush, stroking with open enmity
The parts that make the whole.

Drifting through the fogs of amnesia,
Becalmed in tune, I grasp at strands
To tie, ropish and finally they take
The strain. Touch down. Words are simple.

Divulgence

Seeing each other in ourselves
The same nonchalant gait with
One leg crossed over the other,
Toes pointing downward, her arm
Taking route to a support and leaning.

The left hand with bare third finger
And the index finger possessed of
Carved silver ring, pleasing to the eye.
Having our eyes in mid-glance
Mild curiosity and the slow

Frenzy of passing strangers, tempered
By the sloth surroundings
Of a supermarket. At a quarter to ten.
She must have worked late
With nowhere else to go

Except the aisles of Safeways
Waiting to see herself in me and
Wondering if nothing else was noticed.
But nobody seemed to care that
We had the same taste in bread.

Entitled Interest

Shapes and mis-matched hopes
Bubble up, a distant fountain spray.
Drops of water rain down upon
My haven bound eyes.
Soothing – easing the pain.

Becoming lost in sentiment
Is dangerous, yet I cannot move.
Caught in headlights, startled child,
The trap is beauty,
Infatuation the bloodied spike.

And after trying to explain when
Words become a waste; I'm breached,
Rocks tumbling, crashing with dust.
When focused on every waking thought
She is in my dreams.

Close Company

I reside over a tepid Bank Holiday
Whose sun did not belong to me.

Maybe those kids screaming their innocence
In the distance can lay claim to it
But suddenly all that sounds overhead
Is the jumbo, those inside are
Nearer the sun so perhaps they choose
To reach out, engulfing the flames
Tying close to the chest keeping hearts warm.

Maybe the guy working on the veg
In his kitchen has had a good one
But then I look again and neighbours
Have drawn curtains against the hot stare.
They seemed to have been psyched out,
Too much blistering so time to call it a day,
Hiding within shadow blessed lounges.

It's so fucking lazy and so am I
With no air to breathe.
But then again my chimes clench fists of sound
As wind turns them, lethargic bells.
They hang from the window where
I peer for the first time on the light
Of a communal garden, which is empty of course.

Maybe the close associations prove right
In the end and this blasted sunlight
Purges all before in mighty waves of
Cleansing heat. Heat that will soon
Turn those fat leaves brown.
Heat that will eventually turn the grass
Carpet into threadbare hay.

Tossing spent stalks to the tepid days
Which follow and that I follow in their wake.

Feeling the Fleeting Moments

Plant a seed and it will grow
To touch many people and those
Who lie in the open, awaiting the
Shining lights, reflective and responsible
For the colours in their world,
Patchwork quilt, sewing the strands.

Shall I rhyme in order to make reason
To those who believe castles in the sand
Remain steadfast in the test of time?
Do the words of wise ones and teachers
From the past make light the problems
Of today, or do we all just let it happen?

Here before you lies my instincts, unfettered
By constant demands, cacophony of sound.
Make sense of your desires, my
Dreams will keep me alive and in doing so
Open the eyes and doors within my mind,
Much like yours, anatomy of a kaleidoscope.

Birds

hear them
what utter freedom
standing as the sun peeps out
through a mash of clouds
what do they rejoice in?
warmth
light
security in
flying

Brief Interludes

What sign adheres to this world within a world?
Time to leave, to run with speed to safety,
To pluck the truth from brief interludes.

This makes you whole and if when alone you are
Done with thoughts that form with bliss, the crystalline,
You gasp what breath is left and grasp

The sides which stick, to slow, to wind in circles the
Depths of you, to let go and shine then keep
The close abundance of your submission.

At times of release you are left standing,
You see it all, that static mirror that
Quiet reflection, freeze-framed flight

The winged passage as clear as those pearls of life,
Those waves to break silently upon your shore
Cleansing the image, the august, momentary

Loss which comes as eyes are lifted, opened
Wide to flinch against the glaring surround.
It parches and with no hiding place

You surrender to memory, the path we walked the words
We spoke yielding steps along the way.
What canopy of cloud, what rooftop

Song those birds cried a tenor to the music tones
Of sea and sky, yet whispered softly, carried far.
Carried far until spilled out, you chorus all

Above and before the glistening, flesh hewn shield,
The mighty armour to keep safe what's
Locked inside alone and drifting.

Stop and hear, stop and see, cease and feel
At once the suit that fits you best then
Return by climbing high and past

The tide leaving the waters behind for they are deep and at
Their heart a cloying truth that repels -
We touch and with brief interlude

Are born.

Not Awake Yet

It was the aura of self-beliefs descending,
The tangible efforts of understanding why
That marked the solemn ring.

Mostly mawkish, all tainted with the gruesome
Need for information, the tale to tell around
The dinner table, listeners

Hung on every word, dripping with the
Matter of fact, the unfortunate scene and
The broken image bleeding.

For hours it went on with sirened,
Mock pall bearers, siphoned traffic
With craning necks all

Eager, all curious to view, only seeing
The huge lorry; the hammer encroaching
Possessing such frailties as a bicycle.

Being down there the atmosphere was
True, quiet astonishing and the
Instinctive regret second

Nature among the figures of authority,
Moving silently, speaking softly, all
Resigned, all knowing.

The Victim was never seen and so with
Justice lay cocooned within the bag merely
A number now, crumpled,

Leaving the forlorn signature of
Passing so life's blood pooled and ran
Down a small decline.

It too is gone now, wiped away and forgotten,
Washed then cleansed from ensuing eyes and so
Arrested from the witness minds.

Procreate Off

What is this affliction that attires me
In a shoddy suit?
I skip daily only to trip,
Then they look, to be sure
The bumbling fool has rejected the game.

Feeling egged on to pastures green in
Wanton lust, wiggling with intensity
More common in ripening baboons.
But why joke? I'm screwed.
Or at least I wish I could be.

Remedial Parting

Nets lisp over the window sill
Push against curtains flapped
And retarded by weight.

There is the notion toward
Each outer edge, open windows,
The fanlight should be open too

Bringing the motion to the
Middle ground, where
Stability resides, happy times.

Gusts dictate the play of
Movement and noise utters
Recompense safety in action.

Merge into a well-piled room
Clap the hands and hear
An echo, bouncing, connected

To its own vibration.
And then the chimes, wind
Fluted artists drowning in

The gales that blow, no mercy.
May as well smile, may
As well take what little

Has been given, options
To accept more ill considered
The palate too unyielding.

Pale Sun Shining

Sacrifice is sincerity of loss and who are
We to make the next man bleed?
That value of tenacity lies in broken parts
And the broken parts lie in small pieces.

Delving deeper sees the whole, the pale
Sun whose eyes cast shadow and shadows
Devour swallowing with envy the parts
That make the whole, so possessing control.

And what choices of reason exist
To mend, to fix, there are none.
The parts are left scattered, strewn toys
While the pieces drift from light to twilight.

Grey Daze

I don't need nothing but remembrance
And a glazed feeling of wastefulness.
Spring showers shatter the pavements
With the sheen of water's banana skin.
Where did I trip?

Coming from the conversation with you
Leaves an emptiness. Peculiar.
We didn't need anything but addiction
And a skin-tight desire to appease.
When will we forgive?

Leaves Are Falling

As leaves are falling,
Do not consider it their end.
To twist and pirouette
Downward, aerial ballet
Then bedding the forest floor.

To see new shoots burst
Out from rusting, golden fires,
Flurries and haste
Fresh lives for continuing
The dance, seasons never end.

And meanwhile the trees,
Whose, embalming peacefulness
Shelters the young ones
Enact the guardianship.
They watch and wait forever.

Oblivion's Soft Pillows

I

Times had been easier with the simplicity of One,
It's hard to accept the virtues of being alone.
Beating fists against the walls of yawning depths
Is the pastime of lunatics living on the fringe.

This picture frame viewed from lead-piped windows
Is soon to change, new shades and pastel colours
Played on by the sun, time moves on,
Dragging baggage and thought to my new kingdom.

II

We drift across our precipices then wonder
Why we tumble, a mis-match of limbs
Broken and tangled, strangling air from lungs
Gasping for respite, gagging for pristine elements

Of Life. And after this lies open fields, rolling
Over hills where I have never laid my back,
Never cast my eyes toward cold blue skies
Whose sun yields in lonely aptitude.

III

Begin afresh and capture the warmth thrown down
By the sun gleaming with residue but
She only gives what she does not need,
Her hot heart beats out a false, generous tattoo.

Meanwhile these bleached streets harbour nothing
Except shed skins, lives of compromise and
Insular desperation clinging to hopes against hope,
Smiling viciously with side-glances.

IV

It is innocence that is constantly misgiven,
Blown to smithereens it falls from grace, with a
Clatter of breaking chains. From lead sackcloth we
Engage open air crisped and piqued, shirking

Against the hygiene. Quiet repose, then with
Garments flung to all sides I run screaming,
Impatient for the coming, lost toward my world,
Trapped within yours and belonging to all others.

The Way of Your Reflection

Seeking shelter in that cold cubby-hole
Burrowed into the small cliffs and
Rumoured canyons before the water,
Looking out and feeling the ghosts.

The pebbled mosaic stretched its yawning
Arms to the left and to the right
Then cut down by hard wood sentries
Gutted with brown, found dying

Between the crystal palm colours and mottled
Peach stones, clouds of warm beige
And grey before the arms that stretched
Enclosed now to embrace.

Then the sea, running a treadmill
Of waves pushing the feet forward.
Salted mud with green washing away
The standing beaches.

I reflected the peace despite the
Mindful fracas of people
Walking past and travelling
With eyes skimming over the surface

Of froth crusted waves outward
To the small boats, islands of
Delicate inaction, sails played with,
Toyed as gently up and down

They flew, gestures toward the
Sea, instruments of tremendous
Paleness conducted and condemned
By cold depths and dank hues.

The sea still ran up the shore
The fanned waves casting breath
Like an old, whipped dawn.
With clouds a mother comfort,

The puffed white mushrooms flossed
With craters meeting sea into the distance,
Laced with union, ornamental bonds
To the horizon.

I reflected all of this, a textured
Postcard from times well gone.
My sea will remain breathless
With its search, the sound of rushing

Stones a voice to the endeavour.
Dismembered beaches lay before
The pink hues and wavered walkways
Carrying people on their voyage.

Click Shutter

It would seem now that you are born
Screaming but soon learn how to yell in silence.
While timid hearts are left to wander,
Back and forth we travel searching
For those whose eyes are mere
Windows with a beautiful view.

And there they parade, glowing with time.
Motionless state of residence,
A collection of icebergs afloat the placid sea.
From coquettish grins to teenage candid camera
The chapters keep nothing by –
A blink then all is here and present.

Now I sit glancing at my reflection
And with it comes the slanting from my eyes
Waking the shudder of passing age.
Strange that I should find it funny
That old photos bring nothing but surprise.
How could I remember each instance?

Our Just Desserts

He came in the mist of night
Dressed dark against the intrigue of shadows.
Amid the blessed bluff of
Near sleep, my eyes must have
Flickered within their shells

And saw him, reaching forward.
He shook my hand and slapped my shoulder
And turned away, looking up
Seeking solace in his
Departure, leaving me.

His touch had been indelible
Casting its echo inside
The hall of me, bereft and clinical.
It left no lingering badness,
Stifled with a loss of words

But enough was done, a gasp then all
Was gone, waking, a sore upon
The vision squandered.
An unknown image of blighted man,
Nightmare's host with rose plucked view.

Quality Time

This morning was fog-strewn, so I was
Told this evening but my eyes like glaciers,
Hard shells above the cold flow had failed to
Notice such niceties of commonplace and circumstance.

Whisper,
Whisper to me now.

I am called, such sweet music resides in
This place, it searches yet the wavering arms
Probe, test, sensuous with a velvet approach
A cradle of sounds but I walk upright, alone.

Whisper,
Whisper to me now.

Surroundings alter, the peripheral is bolder
Than imagined, there, here and real in its
Constant beckoning toward the bulbous offerings,
Better, clearer, richer, seductive and lucid.

Whisper,
Whisper to me now.

I stop short of contemplating, stop short of the
Exposure dreams have and I drip instead.
Steady and composed my glaciers breathe mist and so
This morning was fog-strewn and lived unnoticed.

Whisper,
Whisper to me now.

White Collar Paradise

I do not live here.
The implications of living in
A second floor flat choose
Not to sink in.
Things are quiet around here
And affluence provides
The stars with a chance to shine.
Noticing two free
Car park spaces while leaning
From a window, smoking my
Cigarette in the dead of night,
The biting sensation
At the back of the throat
Is the only thing that
Seems real.

wilting flower

directions and boundaries and the return to
the big smoke begins with my feet down stairs
and being where I am now is a marker
for the journey through hard railed suburbs
creeping with volume and reaching like the
arteries fed from the city's heart, pumping blood
full of the people full the people bleeding
dry the bodice of tall towers crackling

phone lines busy with business chirruping birds
nonsensical and foreign tongues lashing the decks
of commerce modernisation new languid flowing
like oceans and currents breathed to life
through the surface of the pen laughing with
a madman hurry rush painting a picture the
rocking motion of travel coursing between a
labyrinth of ageing brick wrinkled distorted

with you in between and focused in train
windows black this time of day and year
and you smiled and the sound of your face
splintering drowned the chaos of my heart
struggling I saw a feral cat hindered with a
broken paw padding toward a haven in grass
banks but really I was glad to look away glad
to hide a face within your broken hands

Relentless

Days fill up and I had doubted
Them as storms diminished the
High born terms of their haze.

They have passed away to be replaced
By the meagre supply dredged up
Belonging to the razored crown in the sky.

Succumb but then question why
The nature of surrender is release –
For the air to be still as tombs.

There is nothing beyond, at least nothing
Truly real but festered imagination
Pushing past the clouds that reign

With murky depth subdued and heavy
Hanging close to our world, enclosing
A myth the legend well thumbed.

And yet the days remain and cry for
No-one whether given or taken,
Full or empty they remain just days.

And the mosaics they paint are the lives
They harbour, with our dreams pushing past
Those clouds to the clarity and blue beyond.

Light Show and Drawn Curtains

Reside inside an island of calm
Wake up and tire, tire of waiting
For the self-life to expire.
I still spend my time housed within
That moonlight, so alive tonight,
Matronly white, true silver conspired

By empty skies that fill to the brim
The cup of night, still and fresh,
Pristine as a baby's first voice.
The call is echoed and these tendrils
Reach from points of origin called
Stars, specks and grains of sand lie

Beached and their projection of light
A million years in age washes, laps and
Slips from my grasp as I remain reaching
For this slippery might lathered with the
Distance of crossed voids, caresses
All before it while time's tide watches.

And keeps watch with a parent's eyes
That baby's cry is armoured, so
With armour of need and the clinging
Posse of dark light those far off
Suns burn bright and burn heated promise
Of travel through hearts, through minds

And through me.

In Two Parts the Tale

We walked as journeymen through the
Turrets of pathways, swathes of farmland
Obliged our step until a crescent was mounted.
And looking out I saw a sea of fields
In storm before us a wave of corn.

Our two dogs wheeled away in haphazard
Formation, following noses through iron clad
Stems rigid with harvest rusted with growth.
Flying from cover, with no gun to capture
The moment the bird was safe.

And so was I, a refugee upon this
Sea of fields lost but no longer
Searching for home the womb of
Four walls a prison soon enough.
And memories fade and their fading is

A key to a lock previously indisposed.
Our two dogs returned. Then flew again.
The parting of their movement
Enough to disclose the meaning
Of their intent, playful, nosing without working.

And so I turned to return, my companion
Agreed then with strides to match the
Careless ploughs we walked as journeymen.
Down through the fields where we were small,
Down to cross a fence where we were high again.

And looking out I saw my sea of fields.
Still. No whisper of wind. No clamour
Of action and with no thoughts to refuse
My longing I turned inside. Still.
No whisper of wind. Two dogs spent by my side.

Green and Living

A garden alive is a garden fulfilled.
A chorus of birds. Imprecise. Perfect.
Daffodils. Blue thing.
Freshly planted roses.
And voices, belonging to people.
You hear, though not what they say.
A spinning stone upon a roof.
Even motor cars.
The sun is shining too.
There are no clouds, you see.

A Prayer For Solitude

The days will come and then
They will pass again.
And with them, the sinew of time,
Brutal in its application of truth
For truth is as the warm breeze
Washed across the gulf of heaven,
The food of Gods and for the
Souls by their side the breath
Of servitude and humility.

Alight the ride and place your
Faltering steps with caution.
Wind your way and forsake
The need for self but that
Which is the true Self must
Be fed with what gusts and
Plays between the worlds above.
For if they are there, they will
Show you the path within.

Breathing In and Asking

The strains of South London greet me
As I sit, perched on the ledge.
What golden lights fleck the varying
Distances to be breached, warming

The homes with the comfort some never have?
Feeling scattered as dust ruptured
This world is intransigent and evening
Gloom perpetuates our dismembered havens.

What is expected by those behind the
Sirens I hear in the distance?
What is known by the hiding couple
Loping through long grasses safe inside

Their precious humdrum defences?
What may they protect – I for one can see
Them, butchering with meat cleaver eyes
The privacy that cloaks them as paper blanket?

Why should these delicate effects break
Upon my shore? Mimicked by the
Drone of nearby traffic, the petrol driven
Waters do nothing to appease.

Evercasting

If ever the sun would appear golden, it is now.
And even so, she fades, lisping out
Catching the dragon's breath for one final wheeze,
Leaving the window bare as stones.

Western breezes conclude the passing
While the settling scene ambles precociously.
Our star winks once more, a panelled
Door brethren to the orange glow.

This is how we should glimpse at glory:
Broadcasts thrown amid all storms with
Nothing but feelings and tinkered emotions
To play with against the wholesome all.

Giving Away

The Big Smoke swarms and the glistening shrapnel
Of cars weave against the swirl of fumes
Adding to these pastel shadings where a clock, cool and ticking,
Up toward the ceiling sheds time as a skin
Giving away the source

Of these days that begin in the Southern Hemisphere;
So God's banner sweeps across lands and seas
Whether cloistered with cloud or not, warming the rocks,
Blessing the waters, breeding the lives beneath the sky,
Giving away this light

As they walk, or crawl, or swim, or fly but only
In one place do they stand then fall, this home this haven -
Turn back toward your world, your fingerprints are of
This unique place, it lies forgotten and alone this sapphire,
Giving away our sun and

All she has and all she hosts, that sweeping
Banner, the fleeting wings, the streamlined fin,
The inching colony and finally a walking man all
Carved to the same tattoo, all etched within touched alive,
Giving away this life.

Home Improvements

New perspectives but the same horizon limits the visions
Of hope, rambling on with a drunkard's step.
Spying upon your sun, striking through clouds,
Whose brutish muscles hang heavy with rain...
Adds up to not much at all inside.
Immediate clichés can only spring to mind.

Drive on completing the mundane
And don't think twice until, while lying back,
Look outward; try to seek what is inside.
Through the window are the same shadows
No longer bleak with piercing, sharp contours
But only soft black against fuzzy grey.

Who needs it? The utter waging of life,
Letting slip desires to those you reckon on trusting.
Rearrange the room, sweating with energy, salt
Water washing away dust airing the prison,
Keeping tight the tale, that warm comfort of a home.
Tie off, sit back, smoke one endless cigarette.

Returning to the pay packet laden with bills,
Contemplating the necessary, bowing to the heat
Of harsh suns that gift neither light nor harvest,
This assurance of presence - the mother of prediction.
Chase after your stars, whoever you are,
While the jesters roam, parading with clowns.

Official Flirtation

I sit here doing nothing and in
Doing nothing appear removed
From myself and the others who
Whisper their sentiment.

To me they seem fathomless,
Remote beyond redemption
As near yet as impenetrable
As those hung clouds

Overhead, distressing what would
Otherwise be a proper day.
Instead it broods as I do,
Content with the weather-bound

Furrows in the sky and
Happy to know that after a
Scratched phone call we
Remain unseen and untouched.

Old Guy

I'd turned and the nagging element
Revealed it, some old guy.
Some old guy with wrinkles, weathered
Rock burns called character.

Such strength – I must have been
Only a wisp of breeze to him,
Adding to the contours, delicately,
They mount up become the wrinkles.

Dinner; fine cutlery, salt and pepper,
Napkin, glass of wine with bread roll,
Unbuttered, its knife unused
And then his spectacles, like the old guy

Removed and to one side, to me, the
Precision was immaculate.
Seeing the scene at last I found the lynchpin,
The necessity; the old guy.

Parchment 'N' Paper

Distance is singular; it sits comfortably nearer than possible,
One of those sublime qualities, one of those moments similar
To the perfect timing of song to match the instant mood.
Mood is the measurement of distance whose length

Is stretched by you and you alone, empty shelf,
Out of reach an enticing morsel while so near to touch.
But the recoil stinks, reeks of blanched gun-powder
The shot having been fired, the shell hollow and spinning to target

Covering the distance in one stride, God how it cuts,
Slicing through this useless day; this hung and driven
Time of light with blankets or barriers or walls of time.
It's up to you and the distance cast, calmly measured, a

Good measure, with good times, the good life, all good thoughts,
No good riddance, every good choice, fulsome good love, wholesome good faith
In me, in you and in the days of time and light and the
Times of life, our hearts, our souls, goodnight, goodbye.

Petulance and Angels

To give nothing is to sacrifice
The pleasure of opening the door.
To have nothing is to sacrifice
The weight of key and lock.

To have nothing to sacrifice
Is to hold within the heart purity.
To give that heart and surrender
Is to hold within your hands everything.

To love some but not at all
Would be the wind without the rain.
To love all and some in all
Would be the storm within your grasp.

To find hope and then abuse with desire
Is to seek the harvest before the spring.
To gain hope within the whim of knowing
Is to sew the seed then witness life.

Unfinished Business

It was a timid day outside
And the tree however small
Came with open arms to the light.
Green was turned white and purity
Sprayed wide to catch the might

Of the sun, though lying about its
Distance for the cold out there
Gave meaning and while
Alone within the cushioned chamber
I call a life there were trials.

Latitudes called faith have proven
True, so with a cripple's lithe
Tones I stumbled on - a hazard on
A long leash, breathing in only you
For then all other air had gone.

Depth. And a possessive calm that
Had brought nothing but desire.
Yet in that live ocean we lived
With the sound of collapsing waves,
With nothing else to give our

Journey and the white shock
Of unfinished business. Brought upon
Without temperance, issues wrought
Within the world we live now, the
Lustful destruction and the love we sought.

To Love A Lady

To find a love so pure, so uncoloured
By the outside that it lies embedded within your heart,
To find its weight bears down relentlessly
Is a cruel and painful barb to resist.
To long for its touch though never to feel
The lustful agony that taints a withered rose.

To look once more upon her face was heaven,
But for a brief moment memories peeled, their softness divine.
She is a mother now, more graceful so
Yet within her still is all that I once loved.
Our destinies always rest on a knife-edge,
And are balanced by the winds, by the lights and by the dove.

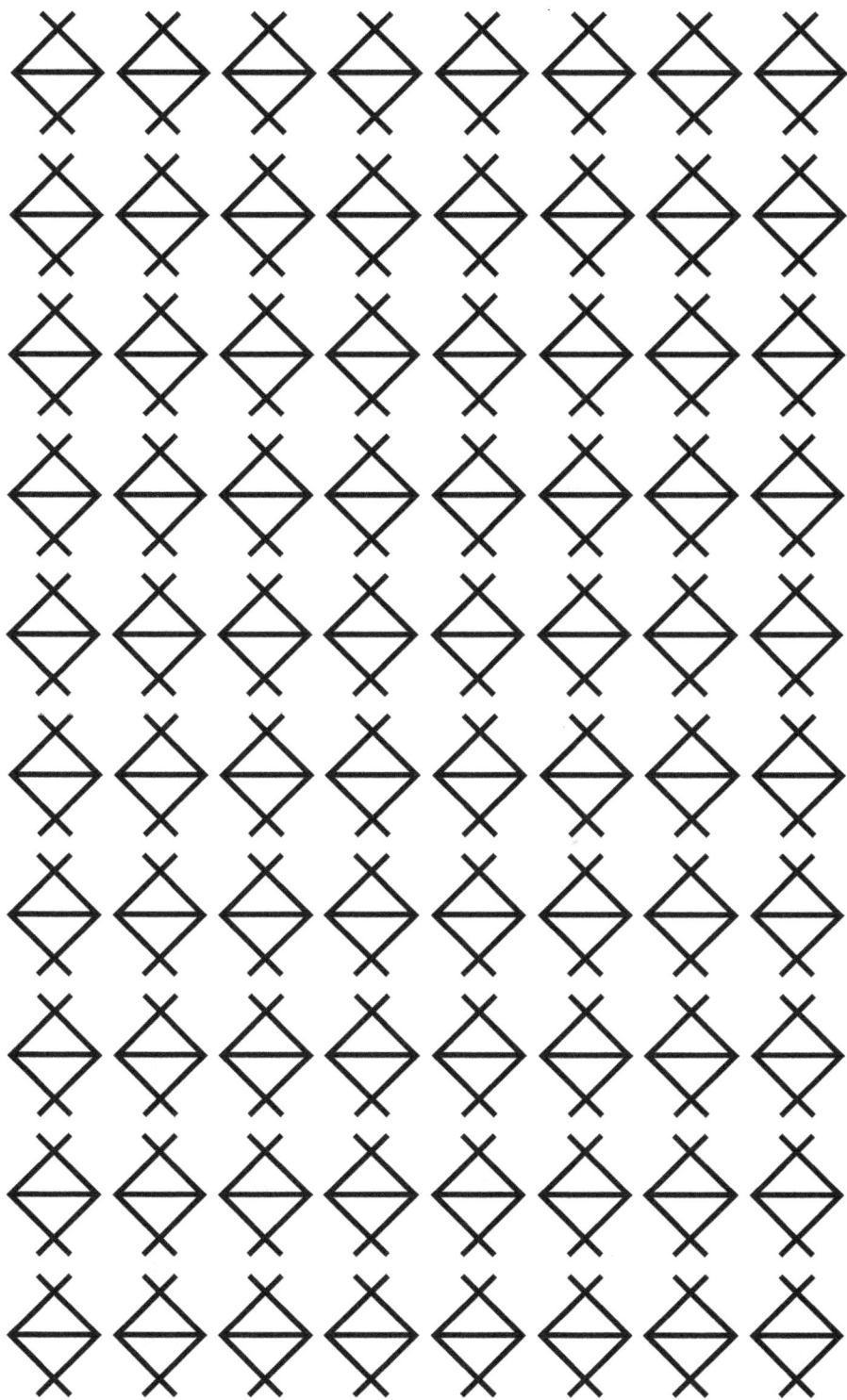

Other Poetry Books Published by Totem

People, Pyramids & Piccadilly
by Ramses Sidrak

Seven Horns Elegy
by Ishmael Annobil

Ethiop
by Ishmael Annobil

AR–K2
by Maurice Jackson

www.ingramcontent.com/pod-product-compliance
Lightning Source LLC
Chambersburg PA
CBHW022343040426
42449CB00006B/697